Reconstr
Characters in the Gospels

Cornelis Bennema
London School of Theology

GROVE BOOKS LIMITED
RIDLEY HALL RD CAMBRIDGE CB3 9HU

Contents

1 Issues in Character Studies 3

2 Theory: An Approach to Character Reconstruction 6

3 Practice I: Sample Character Studies 12

4 Practice II: A Sample Character Across Narratives 21

5 A Final Word 26

Notes 27

First Impression March 2021
ISSN 1365-490X
ISBN 978 1 78827 155 4

1 Issues in Character Studies

Every story has characters that drive the plot; otherwise, there is no story. When we read a story, we inevitably piece together characters from the text to follow the story. No character is presented to the reader whole, so we engage in 'character reconstruction.' The author constructs a character and disperses information about that character in the text. The reader reconstructs that character by gathering scattered information from the text and piecing together a mental picture of that character (although the reader does not merely decode what the author has encoded). While some readers do so intuitively, others use a particular approach.

I have two reasons for formalizing the process of character reconstruction. First, since every reader engages in character reconstruction, it is important to ask how we go about it or what we should be looking for. Characters in the New Testament have been the subject of literary-critical study since the 1970s, but there is still no agreed approach to character. For example, readers refer easily to 'doubting Thomas,' but to what extent does the adjective 'doubting' capture the way John's gospel portrays him? Is it just a general impression or can we find specific ways of examining John's construction of Thomas's character?

Secondly, a uniform approach to character reconstruction is beneficial because it enables the comparison of characters both within and across narratives. If we use an open-ended approach, where people choose from a plurality of methods and approaches, we may get an interesting set of character reconstructions but no common basis for comparison, dialogue and evaluation.[1] Or, if I use one approach to reconstruct the character of Peter in Mark's gospel but another approach for Peter in John's gospel, I cannot profitably compare these two characterizations.

Criteria for a Suitable Approach

While I will explain and showcase my approach to reconstructing characters, I am not claiming this is the only or best approach. But neither do I regard all approaches to be equally effective or fruitful. I propose three criteria for selecting a suitable approach to character reconstruction.

First, an approach must be *sufficiently sophisticated* or *comprehensive* to account for the variety of characters in New Testament narrative to avoid oversimplification. Even a superficial reading of the gospels will reveal that the characters are far from homogeneous. While the well-known categories of 'flat' and 'round' characters remain useful, they are too reductionistic because not every character neatly fits into these categories.[2] Hence, we need an approach that can sufficiently distinguish between the various characters and account for their diversity.

Secondly, an approach must be *sufficiently economic* to be feasible or practical. While the binary categories flat and round lack nuance, some approaches have become too detailed to be useful, using eight to ten categories to analyze characters. An efficient approach to character should not be too complicated but do enough to allow a meaningful character analysis.

Thirdly, an approach must be *sufficiently quantifiable* or *evaluative* to 'measure' and compare characters within and across narratives. Although some approaches can measure several aspects of character, such as coherence, complexity, transparency or development, readers are often left with unrelated categories of character information. This suggests that we need to collect and combine data about characters to assess their totality and make them suitable for comparison.

Ancient and Modern Characterization

When it comes to the gospels most characters are viewed as flat or types

We cannot simply assume that characterization in ancient and modern literature is the same. Regarding antiquity, many perceive character in the Old Testament, where characters can be complex and develop (think of Jacob, Samson, David or Jonah), to be radically different from that in ancient Greek literature, where characters are supposedly flat or ethical types. Aristotle's notion of character in particular has been immensely influential on New Testament scholars. Aristotle viewed character as fixed and subordinate to the plot; character simply reveals (moral) choice (*The Poetics*, 6.7–24). His concept of character corresponds to the modern category 'flat' or 'type.' Many people also sharply distinguish between modern literature with its psychological, individualistic approach to character and ancient characterization where characters seemingly lack personality or individuality. When it comes to the gospels, therefore, most characters are viewed as flat or types, such as impulsive Peter, Judas the betrayer or Thomas the doubter. Although some have come to see greater complexity in the gospel characters, much of the stereotypical thinking remains.

I have four objections to viewing New Testament characters through an Aristotelian lens. First, such an approach neglects the possible or probable influence of Hebraic characterization on the New Testament authors' construction of characters. Secondly, Aristotle's view of character in Greek tragedy is not representative of all ancient Greek literature; ancient Greek characters could be more complex or round. Thirdly, many New Testament characters are unlike Graeco-Roman stock characters and display various degrees of 'roundness.' Fourthly, the audience of a Greek drama evaluates only the protagonist as a model to be emulated or avoided, while readers of New Testament narratives are also invited to evaluate the other characters. In other words, characters in Greek drama exist for the sake of the protagonist (they assist the characterization of the protagonist), but in the New Testament they exist for the sake of the reader.

This led me to re-evaluate ancient characterization and develop a new approach to character in New Testament narrative.[3] I began by examining concepts of character in ancient Hebrew and Greek literature as well as modern narrative, arguing that although there are differences in characterization, these are differences in *emphasis* rather than kind. It is therefore better to speak of *degrees* of characterization along a continuum.[4] Both ancient and modern literature can portray flat and round, static and dynamic characters, although in modern narrative character is far more developed and psychologized. This implies that we can use insights from modern literary methods to analyze characters in ancient literature. I then articulated a comprehensive, three-dimensional approach to character in New Testament narrative, consisting of (i) character in text and context; (ii) character analysis and classification; and (iii) character evaluation and significance. I will first explain my approach and then show how it works.

2 Theory: An Approach to Character Reconstruction

Character in Text and Context

The first aspect of my approach is to study character in text and context, using information in the text and other sources. The truism 'There are no characters without a text' would indicate that characters are limited to the world of the text and therefore the reader's character reconstruction is based solely on the information in the text. I think this is an inaccurate deduction and I suggest that we can go *beyond* the text for the reconstruction of character. I regard the New Testament narratives as non-fictional in nature, having reference to real events and people in history. This means we can fill the gaps in the narrative with knowledge of the sociohistorical context of the first-century Mediterranean world. Too often narrative critics restrict themselves to the text of the gospels and the narrative world these evoke, effectively reading the gospels as fictional narratives disconnected from reality.

At the same time, in presenting their characters, the gospel authors were selective and flexible in using their sources. For example, John the Baptist appears in the Synoptic gospels as a rough-hewn figure preaching a baptism of repentance whereas John's gospel presents him as an eloquent witness for Jesus. The gospels probably fit best in the genre of the ancient Graeco-Roman biography. As such, they would be truthful narrations of Jesus' life and teachings, though the speech of characters would often be paraphrases rather than the literal words. While the gospel authors may have exercised such literary freedom, what matters is that the reader need not doubt their credibility; they would not have created fictitious characters. Thus, the historicity of the characters in the gospels does not exclude the possibility that the authors used a legitimate degree of freedom to portray them.

We must also consider the extent of the reader's knowledge because the reader reconstructs character. I use the concept of a modern reader who has adequate knowledge of the first-century world and can give a plausible explanation for the ancient sources they presume. We should not assume that the only source available to the reader is the text they are reading. The reader's character reconstruction can be influenced by other texts where the same character features.

Consider the calling of Peter in the Synoptics. A reader with access to just the Gospel of Mark or Matthew might see vast gaps in the text when, without any explanation, Peter impulsively (perhaps even naïvely) leaves his trade and family to follow Jesus, whom he has never met before (Mark 1.16–18; Matt 4.18–20). A reader who also knows Luke's account will note several differences. First, in Luke the healing of Peter's mother-in-law (Luke 4.38–39) occurs *prior* to Peter's calling (Luke 5.1–11), whereas Mark and Matthew have these in reverse order. So, in Luke Peter already knows Jesus *prior* to his call. Secondly, Luke 5.1–11 expands the Markan / Matthean account of Peter's calling and reduces the textual gaps. For example, while the Markan / Matthean Jesus plucks Peter away from his profession with the promise to make him a 'fisher of people,' the Lukan Jesus draws Peter with an object lesson—a miraculous catch of fish—to help him visualize the nature and magnitude of his new vocation. In effect, Luke has enhanced Peter's characterization and provided a stronger rationale for Peter radically abandoning trade and family.

Character Analysis and Classification

The second component in character reconstruction is to analyze and classify the New Testament characters. For this I draw on the classification of Yosef Ewen, who uses three continua upon which a character may be situated:[5]

- *Complexity*: characters range from those displaying a single trait to those displaying a complex web of traits, with degrees of complexity in between.
- *Development*: characters range from those who show no development to those who are fully developed. Development is *not* simply the reader becoming aware of an additional trait in a character later in the narrative or a character's progress, for example, in understanding Jesus. Instead, development is revealed in the character's ability to surprise the reader. When a new trait replaces another or does not fit neatly into the existing set of traits, the implication is that the character has changed.
- *Inner life*: characters range from stock figures who are seen only from the outside (their minds remain opaque) to those who are transparent, allowing us to see the character's thoughts, emotions and motivations.

In chapter one, I proposed that more can be done in terms of character analysis, so I have introduced two enhancements to Ewen's model. The first is to *refine* his classification by marking each continuum by *degree*, creating a sliding scale instead of a polar scale.[6] Instead of a continuum of complexity with 'simple' and 'complex' at each end, I will use one that marks the degree of complexity—'none', 'little', 'some' and 'much'. This refinement will facilitate a comparison of the various characters.

To avoid being left with three disconnected continua, the second enhancement is to *supplement* Ewen's model with an *aggregate* continuum that indicates the character's total degree of characterization. In other words, after plotting a character along the three continua of complexity, development and inner life, I plot the resulting character on an aggregate continuum of degree of characterization as (i) an agent; (ii) a type; (iii) a character with personal features or personality; or (iv) an individual or person. I do not use the terms 'individual' and 'person' in the modern sense of an autonomous individual, but to refer to a 'collectivist identity' or 'group-oriented personality' where the individual identity is embedded in a larger group or community (as was the case in ancient cultures). The results of the character analysis can be presented in the following table:

Character	Complexity	Development	Inner Life	Degree of Characterization
Character 1	0	0	0	agent
Character 2	–	0	0	type
Character 3	+	–	–/+	personality
Character 4	++	+	+	toward individual
Character 5	++	++	+	individual

Key: 0 = none, – = little, + = some, ++ = much

I avoid quantifying the terms 'little', 'some' and 'much' but position a character on each continuum in relation to other characters. While some may question such an intuitive approach and prefer more precise definitions or objective criteria for what constitutes 'little', 'some' and 'much', I think this is not achievable. I simply place each character on a continuum proportionate to the other characters, so the character's positioning is always relative.

Character Evaluation and Significance

The third aspect of character reconstruction in the gospels is (i) to evaluate the characters' responses to the protagonist; (ii) to consider their role in the plot; and (iii) to determine their significance or representative value for today.[7] Since Jesus is the protagonist in all four gospels and each author seeks to persuade his readers to accept his view of Jesus, the main criterion for evaluating characters in the gospels is therefore their responses to Jesus. Let me explain with reference to John's gospel. I evaluate the characters' responses to Jesus in keeping with *John's* evaluative point of view. As the characters interact with Jesus, John evaluates their responses according to his point of view and communicates this evaluative system to the reader with the intention that the reader embraces it. John's point of view is informed by the purpose and worldview of his gospel. His strategy for achieving the soteriological purpose of writing his gospel (John 20.30–31) is to put various characters on the stage where they interact with Jesus. John wants his readers to evaluate the characters' responses to Jesus and, in turn, respond to Jesus themselves. John's worldview only allows for two responses to Jesus—acceptance and rejection—and hence his evaluative point of view also allows for two options—adequate and inadequate belief responses. An adequate belief response is a sufficiently true understanding of Jesus in terms of his identity, mission and relationship with God, resulting in a commitment to Jesus in discipleship. While I cannot determine how much authentic understanding is sufficient, I can discern *John's* evaluation of the character's response.

Although John's evaluative point of view allows for just two options (adequate and inadequate), the characters' responses to Jesus form a broad spectrum. For example, Nicodemus shows sympathy, signs of faith, and ambiguity. The Samaritan woman is cooperative, makes cognitive progress, professes belief and testifies about Jesus. The invalid at the pool is first obedient and sides with Jesus but soon turns against him. Mary of Bethany shows progressive understanding, devotion and servanthood. So how do such diverse responses fit into the binary categories of belief and unbelief, adequate and inadequate? I suggest that the Johannine characters reflect the *human* perspective, representing the whole gamut of human responses, while from a *divine* perspective these responses are ultimately deemed to be acceptance or rejection. For John, the divine reality is that the world and its people are enveloped in darkness and do not know God—they are 'from below' (John 1.5; 8.23). To dispel this darkness and people's lack of divine knowledge, Jesus came to reveal God and bring people into a life-giving relationship with himself and God. When the Johannine characters encounter Jesus, their responses range across a broad spectrum, but because they operate within John's dualistic framework, their responses will eventually (and perhaps only at the end of their lives or at the *parousia*) be distilled or crystallize to the basic categories of acceptance and rejection.

The Johannine characters represent the whole gamut of human responses

We can also consider the characters' relation to the plot, where plot is the logical and causal order of events in a narrative. Due to the influence of Aristotle's concept of character as type and subordinate to the plot, some people view characters simply as plot functionaries. Consequently, characters have often been unnaturally flattened. If, however, plot and character are equally important and interdependent, there is value in examining the character's role in the plot. Let me elaborate with reference to Mark's gospel this time. The Markan plot revolves around conflict, caused by the proclamation of the good news of Jesus' identity and mission, and the various responses of people. The plot is shaped by the author's aim to persuade the audience to believe the good news that Jesus is the Christ and Son of God (Mark 1.1, 14–15) and commit to discipleship. Several characters advance the plot of Mark's narrative because they function as examples of faith and discipleship, and the extent to which these characters respond to Jesus and reveal aspects of true discipleship is the extent to which they advance the plot. For example, in contrast to the disciples (Mark 6.52; 8.19–21), the Syrophoenician woman understands the significance of leftovers and advances the plot in that she helps reveal that Jesus' mission will extend beyond Israel's ethnic and geographical borders (Mark 7.27–29).

Reconstructing characters from the text is a hermeneutical process that merges two horizons—that of the historical-narratological world of the text and that of the contemporary world of the reader. This creates the possibility for two-way communication where the characters can influence the reader and thus have a role or impact beyond the narrative. In short, characters have a representative value for today. As the reader evaluates the characters in the narrative according to the author's point of view and purpose, it might lead the reader to seek to emulate some characters (those who align themselves with the author's perspective) and avoid others (those whose behaviour is unacceptable from the author's perspective). In other words, we should reflect on how the gospel characters have representative value for readers in other contexts and times.

Collating Results

The results of our character reconstruction can be collated in the following table of character descriptors.

Name of Character	
Narrative Appearances	
Origin	Birth, Gender, Ethnicity, Nation/City
	Family (Ancestors, Relatives)
Upbringing	Nurture, Education
External Goods	Epithets, Reputation
	Age, Marital Status
	Socioeconomic Status, Wealth
	Place of Residence/Operation
	Occupation, Positions Held

	Group Affiliation, Friends
Speech and Actions	Interaction with the Protagonist
	Interaction with Other Characters
Death	Manner of Death, Events after Death
Character Analysis	Complexity
	Development
	Inner Life
Character Classification	Degree of Characterization
Character Evaluation	Response to the Protagonist
	Role in the Plot
Character Significance	Representative Value

The top half of the table (from 'narrative appearances' to 'death') contains various character descriptors that correspond to the basic topics found in ancient Graeco-Roman rhetorical handbooks.[8] This information is gathered in the first step, the study of character in text and context through exegesis or a close reading of the text. The bottom half of the table contains aggregate information about the characters in terms of their complexity, development, inner life, degree of characterization, evaluation and significance as I outlined above. This meta level of characterization is essential for determining how characters relate to each other within a narrative. The two parts of the table thus reflect the fusion of the ancient and modern horizons in the reconstruction of character.

I contend that this uniform approach meets the criteria stated in chapter one. I must stress that the uniform aspect of our approach applies mainly to the second step where I collate metadata about a character. In the first step, a close reading of the text to analyze a character in relation to ancient topics, a plurality of approaches is possible. While a close reading of the text will always be the first step in character reconstruction, it must be a guided reading focused on identifying particular aspects of character. Based on such reading, we can collect aggregate data about a character to facilitate a comparison of characters within and beyond narratives.

3 Practice I: Sample Character Studies

A theory is only as good as it works. So, we will put our theory to the test in two ways. In this chapter, we will analyze different characters in the same narrative—Thomas, the chief priests and Judas in John's gospel. In the next chapter, we will analyze one character across different narratives, namely Mary, the mother of Jesus, in the four gospels. We will pay attention to (i) the character's speech and actions; (ii) what other characters and the narrator say about that character; and (iii) relevant information about the first-century world.

Thomas

Character in Text and Context. Thomas is popularly known as doubting Thomas but this is a misleading portrait. He was one of the twelve (John 20.24) and known by the moniker of 'Twin' (John 11.16; 20.24; 21.2). Thomas shows misunderstanding on three occasions. In the first instance, Jesus is in Perea to escape the murderous efforts of the Jerusalem authorities (John 10.31, 39–42). When Jesus suggests that they return to Judea to visit ill Lazarus, his disciples are alarmed (John 11.7–15). Thomas's exclamation, 'Let us also go, that we may die with him' in John 11.16 shows that he partially misunderstands Jesus, fearing that the authorities would kill them. Yet, Thomas's declaration also speaks of courage and loyalty. He seems prepared, perhaps more so than Peter in John 13.37, to lay down his life for his master (see John 15.13) since Jesus does not comment on his suggestion (unlike with Peter). The second instance of Thomas's misunderstanding occurs when Jesus speaks of his imminent departure, assuring his disciples that they know where he is going. Thomas's reaction, however, reveals that he does not grasp what Jesus says (John 14.1–5). Thomas's third misunderstanding has to do with his need to see and touch the risen Jesus (John 20.25). Although Jesus graciously fulfils Thomas's demand, he encourages him (and others) toward a belief that is less dependent on the tangible (John 20.27–29). Like Mary Magdalene in John 20.17, Thomas appears not to have understood Jesus' teaching in John 14.15–23 that Jesus' ongoing presence would be spiritual rather than physical.

For reasons unknown to us, Thomas is absent that Sunday evening when Jesus appears to the disciples (John 20.24). When they recount their experience, Thomas declares that he will have to see and touch Jesus for himself in order to believe (John 20.25). This response has earned him the nickname 'doubting Thomas'—somewhat unfairly. He simply asks for the same first-hand experience of the risen Jesus that the other disciples had (John 20.20). Jesus' rebuke in John 20.29 is not harsh, considering that Mary Magdalene and the disciples had tangible experiences of him. Nonetheless, Thomas's proviso reveals disbelief (he is sceptical about the testimony of the other disciples) and misunderstanding (see above). A week later, Thomas has his own encounter with the risen Lord, one similar in fashion and location to that of the other disciples (John 20.26). Jesus invites Thomas to examine his scars as Thomas had requested while also encouraging him to discontinue his unbelief and believe (John 20.27). Thomas's reply, 'My Lord and my God!' is the Christological climax of the gospel and expresses adequate belief (John 20.28).

Thomas's Characterization. Instead of a doubter, we find a character who displays traits of courage, loyalty and discipleship—even willing to lay down his life for Jesus. Thomas does often misunderstand Jesus but in that he is not unique. Thomas is a realist, displaying a down-to-earth, sometimes questioning, faith in Jesus. His scepticism, however, needs correction, which occurs in John 20.24–28. While Thomas shows no character development, there are a few glimpses into his inner life (sceptical, pragmatic). I thus classify him as a 'type'. Thomas represents the pragmatic person who needs a personal experience of Jesus to believe but who is encouraged to progress toward a belief that is less dependent on such experiences. The real issue was not to believe that Jesus had risen but of believing *someone else's testimony* about this.[9] Thomas's struggle represents the struggle of later generations of believers who have not witnessed the resurrection of Jesus and must depend on others' testimony.[10] Future believers are encouraged to 'see,' that is, encounter, the risen Lord in the eyewitness account of John's gospel and believe (John 19.35; 20.30–31; 21.24). Thomas's demand for a first-hand experience of the risen Jesus advances the plot because it precipitates Jesus' exhortation to later generations to base their faith on trustworthy eyewitness testimony.

Thomas		
Narrative Appearances	11.16; 14.5; 20.24, 26–28; 21.2	
Origin	Birth, Gender, Ethnicity, Nation/City	male
	Family (Ancestors, Relatives)	
Upbringing	Nurture, Education	
External Goods	Epithets, Reputation	Twin
	Age, Marital Status	
	Socioeconomic Status, Wealth	
	Place of Residence/Operation	travels with Jesus
	Occupation, Positions Held	
	Group Affiliation, Friends	the Twelve

Speech and Actions	Interaction with Jesus	committed but misunderstands; pragmatic, sceptical faith
	Interaction with Other Characters	disbelieves others' testimony
Death	Manner of Death, Events After Death	willing to die with Jesus
Character Analysis	Complexity	little complex; multiple traits
	Development	none
	Inner Life	little
Character Classification	Degree of Characterization	type
Character Evaluation	Response to Jesus	eventually adequate belief
	Role in the Plot	he is part of the plot's resolution
Character Significance	Representative Value	pragmatists who desire tangible experiences but are encouraged to rely less on the concrete/physical

The Chief Priests

Character in Text and Context. I regard the chief priests as a *corporate* character, a group that is homogeneous in its identity and behaviour. They are the main leaders of a larger group, called 'the Jews,' which is a composite group of Torah- and temple-loyalists that includes the Pharisees as the influential laity.[11] The chief priests are the temple authorities or 'clergy,' the religious-political authorities who have the power to convene the Sanhedrin on judicial-religious matters. While the Pharisees argue with Jesus on various theological issues (law, sabbath, Moses, Abraham), the conflict between the chief priests and Jesus is more religious-political in nature. They view Jesus as a political threat to their power base, the temple in Jerusalem (see John 11.48).

The chief priests first appear in John 7, together with the Pharisees in a meeting of the Sanhedrin, but the Pharisees are the dominant voice (John 7.32, 45–52). Their second appearance is in John 11–12, towards the end of Jesus' ministry in the feverish aftermath of the raising of Lazarus. There, in another Sanhedrin meeting with the Pharisees, the chief priests come to the fore, plotting Jesus' death because they perceive him as a political threat. The final appearance of the chief priests, now accompanied by 'the Jews,' is in John 18–19 where they orchestrate Jesus' death during his trial before Pilate. With each appearance in the narrative, the chief priests become increasingly vocal and domineering—from being virtually silent (John 7.45–52) to debating (John 11.45–53) to shouting (John 19.6, 15). In John's account, 'the Jews' in general but the chief priests in particular are responsible for Jesus' death.

Character Analysis. The chief priests display several traits. At the Feast of Tabernacles, when people begin to speak of Jesus as the Messiah, the chief priests (and Pharisees) mobilize the temple police to arrest Jesus (John 7.25–32). This shows that they are proactive and alert to threats. Then, the aftermath of Jesus' raising of Lazarus propels the chief priests to drastic action (John 11.45–57). While they are uncertain, anxious and angry, they are also proactive, decisive, organized and have murderous intent. Their resolve to kill Lazarus so they might quell the large number of defecting 'Jews' also shows them to be ruthless and calculating (John 12.10–11). Finally, during Jesus' trial, the chief priests are hostile, violent, exasperated and murderous (John 19.6, 15). They disregard their own religious traditions to secure Jesus' death (John 19.15). In complaining to Pilate about the precise wording of the inscription on the cross, the chief priests appear punctilious and dissatisfied (John 19.21). In sum, the chief priests have multiple traits, indicating a complex corporate character.

In terms of character development, the chief priests are generally consistent in their traits and behaviour. The only instance in which they are able to surprise the reader is in John 19.15. With Pilate continuing to frustrate their efforts to secure Jesus' death, the chief priests finally find a way to force Pilate's hand by questioning his loyalty to the emperor (John 19.12). In return, Pilate decides to extract a heavy price. He taunts them by asking whether he should crucify their king, thus exacting from them their allegiance to Rome (John 19.15). The chief priests sadly choose to sacrifice their religious and national hopes to secure Jesus' death and ensure their own political survival.

The narrative indicates several aspects of the chief priests' inner life. For example, they are upset and anxious about the possible implications of Jesus' raising of Lazarus (John 11.47–48). At first, they are uncertain about what to do (John 11.47–48) but then resolve to kill both Jesus (John 11.53) and Lazarus (John 12.10). Their shouting shows that they are exasperated by Pilate's handling of the case (John 19.6, 15), and their remark to Pilate regarding the inscription on the cross reveals their dissatisfaction (John 19.21). It is unsurprising that aspects of the chief priests' inner life mirror their traits. For example, their frustration with Pilate's taunts is caused by their hostility and murderous intent regarding Jesus; their dissatisfaction with the precise wording of the inscription on the cross arises from (or reveals) their being punctilious.

Characterization of the Chief Priests. We can situate the character of the chief priests on our three continua as follows. They show much complexity and have multiple traits, indicate little development, and reveal some inner life. Considering their degree of characterization, the chief priests are certainly more than a 'type' but show insufficient development and inner life to be considered as 'individual'. So, I classify the resulting character as a 'corporate personality'. That is, as a homogeneous group, the chief priests act as a singular character that shows personality but falls short of individuality. Regarding their corporate or group-oriented personality, the chief priests' identity is embedded in the larger group of 'the Jews'. As for the plot, the chief priests propel it forward significantly through masterminding and precipitating Jesus' death. From John's evaluative point of view, the chief priests' response to Jesus must be evaluated negatively. Regarding the representative value of the chief priests beyond John's narrative world, they could represent (religious) leaders who are so concerned about their status and survival that they are prepared to eliminate those who they perceive as a threat at any cost.

Chief Priests		
Narrative Appearances	7.32, 45; 11.47, 57; 12.10; 18.3, 35; 19.6, 15, 21	
Origin	Birth, Gender, Ethnicity, Nation/City	male
	Family (Ancestors, Relatives)	heads of the high priestly families
Upbringing	Nurture, Education	
External Goods	Epithets, Reputation	
	Age, Marital Status	
	Socioeconomic Status, Wealth	prominent, powerful
	Place of Residence/Operation	temple in Jerusalem
	Occupation, Positions Held	priestly aristocracy
	Group Affiliation, Friends	'the Jews,' Pharisees, temple police
Speech and Actions	Interaction with Jesus	hostile, murderous intentions
	Interaction with Other Characters	dismissive, controlling, manipulative
Death	Manner of Death, Events After Death	
Character Analysis	Complexity	complex; multiple traits
	Development	little
	Inner Life	some
Character Classification	Degree of Characterization	(corporate) personality
Character Evaluation	Response to Jesus	inadequate
	Role in the Plot	advance the plot by planning and executing Jesus' arrest and death
Character Significance	Representative Value	shrewd, ruthless leaders

Judas Iscariot

Character in Text and Context. Judas belongs to Jesus' inner group of disciples (John 6.71; 12.4), in which he is the treasurer (John 12.6; 13.29). Our focus is on the epithets given to Judas: 'devil' (John 6.70), 'betrayer' (John 6.71; 12.4; 13.11; 18.2, 5), 'thief' (John 12.6) and 'son of destruction' (John 17.12).

Devil. When many disciples start defecting, Jesus challenges the twelve on their loyalty to him, but Peter assures him that they will stick with him (John 6.60–69). What Peter does not know, and Jesus reveals, is that even among the twelve there is a devil (John 6.70). This could mean that Judas will side with the devil or that his behaviour resembles that of the devil. The devil's main occupation is to lie and kill (John 8.44). Similarly, Judas lies and, through his betrayal, abets Jesus' killing (John 12.5–6). In fact, Judas will become an instrument of the devil (John 13.2, 27).

Betrayer. The verb translated 'betray' essentially means 'to hand over,' but with reference to Judas the verb always has negative connotations with the force of 'to betray' (John 6.64, 71; 12.4; 13.2, 11, 21; 18.2, 5; 19.11; 21.20). John 18.1–12 describes Judas's specific act of betrayal, handing Jesus over to the Jewish and Roman authorities. With this act Judas aligns himself with 'the Jews' (Jesus' main opponents) and the Roman oppressors. Incidentally, Judas and 'the Jews' are both controlled by the devil (John 8.44; 13.2, 27).

Thief. In John 12.6, John's readers learn that Judas is a thief. That Judas is a thief while also the treasurer only compounds his dishonesty and disloyalty to the group—he betrays their trust. The term 'thief' occurs only here and in John 10. Perhaps John deliberately portrays Judas as a false shepherd whose intention is to steal, kill and destroy. Judas is also a liar or hypocrite, who, with his question in John 12.5, feigns concern for the poor, and that John quickly exposes. In this Judas emulates the devil who is characterized as a liar (John 8.44).

Son of Destruction. When Jesus speaks of Judas and the fulfilment of Scripture in John 17.12, it raises the issue of whether Judas was (pre)destined to be lost, but this seems an overtranslation in many English Bibles. Instead, James Brownson suggests that the phrase 'son of destruction' is a genitive of origin, where the Greek term *apōleia* ('destruction') probably stands for the Hebrew *Abaddon*, a term used for hell (Prov 15.11; 27.20) or hell personified, the devil (Job 28.22).[12] In which case, the reference to Judas as 'son of destruction/hell' corresponds to the earlier description of Judas as 'devil' (John 6.70–71). So, the label 'son of destruction' implies that Judas is an agent of the devil—he belongs to the devil and acts like him.

Negative Development. Apostasy is the defection from Jesus to the opposition, the devil. In John 13.2, we learn that the devil plants the idea of betraying Jesus in Judas's heart. Then, in John 13.18, Jesus speaks of Judas's imminent betrayal as a fulfilment of Psalm 41.9, where David recalls being betrayed by an intimate friend he trusted and had table-fellowship with. In John 13.21–30, a similar scene plays out between Jesus and Judas. While serving to identify

Judas as the betrayer, Jesus' gesture of sharing bread in John 13.26 may also be a last effort to restore fellowship. However, the devil enters into Judas after he takes the piece of bread (John 13.27). Being indwelled by the devil, Judas stands in sharp contrast to the disciples, who are indwelled by the Father and Son (John 14.23). Judas has become a devil or his embodiment (see John 6.70), an apostate who switched his allegiance from Jesus to the devil. John 13 records the tragic defection of Judas in a context that promotes discipleship.

Judas's Characterization. Judas's defection is permanent (unlike Peter's) and denotes apostasy. He ceases to be a disciple of Jesus and becomes a disciple of the devil. Judas mimics the devil's characteristics and behaviour: he lies about his concern for the poor (John 12.5–6); he steals money from the common purse (John 12.6); he aids the arrest and hence the killing of Jesus. He is an instrument and embodiment of the devil. Judas is a complex character whose many traits include betrayal, apostasy, indifference, hypocrisy, unreliability, dishonesty and disloyalty. We have noted several aspects of Judas's inner life: he is indifferent, hypocritical and dishonest (John 12.6); his thoughts are influenced by the devil (John 13.2); and he knows Jesus' habits (John 18.3). Judas shows significant development in that his behaviour shocks the reader as new traits emerge. Being a thief while also the treasurer of the group implies that traits of honesty and reliability are replaced by dishonesty and unreliability. Early on, Jesus reveals that Judas will develop from being his follower to a betrayer (John 6.70–71). When Jesus reiterates this in John 13.21, the disciples are shocked, suggesting that this is an unexpected development. Even in John 13.26–29, the disciples seem too stunned to grasp Jesus' clue to the betrayer's identity. With the shift of allegiance from Jesus to the devil, traits of intimacy and discipleship are replaced by alienation and defection. In short, the catastrophic switch from being a disciple of Jesus to becoming a disciple of the devil and the replacement of traits signify the change in Judas.

Considering the location of Judas's character on the continua of complexity (complex, multiple traits), development (some) and inner life (much), his degree of characterization is high and we can classify the character of Judas as 'individual'. From John's evaluative point of view, Judas must be evaluated negatively. Judas's apostasy was the climax of a gradual, negative development rather than an abrupt event. Judas's betrayal is not limited to the premeditated act of handing Jesus over to the authorities but is a pattern of behaviour that emerged over time. As a thief and then as a defector and apostate, he betrays the trust of Jesus and his fellow disciples. He belongs to Jesus' inner circle of disciples, has an intimate relationship with Jesus, but eventually chooses to join the opposition. At the heart of betrayal is relationship, so Judas is the betrayer as an intimate friend and disciple of Jesus. Judas propels the plot to its climax, in that his key role in Jesus' arrest significantly aids 'the Jews' in killing Jesus. Regarding Judas's significance for today, he represents those who belonged to Jesus but have defected and joined the opposition—the devil.

Judas Iscariot		
Narrative Appearances	6.71; 12.4; 13.2, 26, 29; 18.2–3, 5	
Origin	Birth, Gender, Ethnicity, Nation/City	male, perhaps from Kerioth
	Family (Ancestors, Relatives)	son of Simon
Upbringing	Nurture, Education	
External Goods	Epithets, Reputation	devil, betrayer, thief, son of perdition
	Age, Marital Status	
	Socioeconomic Status, Wealth	
	Place of Residence/ Operation	travels with Jesus
	Occupation, Positions Held	treasurer of the twelve
	Group Affiliation, Friends	the twelve, the devil, ally of 'the Jews' and Romans
Speech and Actions	Interaction with Jesus	disloyal, betrayal
	Interaction with Other Characters	betrays trust of other disciples; aids Jewish police and Romans
Death	Manner of Death, Events After Death	
Character Analysis	Complexity	complex; multiple traits
	Development	some (negative)
	Inner Life	much
Character Classification	Degree of Characterization	individual
Character Evaluation	Response to Jesus	inadequate: betrayal and apostasy
	Role in the Plot	Judas propels the plot to its climax
Character Significance	Representative Value	followers of Jesus who become disloyal to Jesus and others

The following table shows how these characters relate to one another in terms of their characterization. If we were to plot all Johannine characters, we would discover the rich variety of John's cast of characters.[13]

Character	Complexity	Development	Inner Life	Degree of Characterization
Thomas	–	0	–	type
Chief Priests	++	–	+	(corporate) personality
Judas Iscariot	++	+	++	individual

Key: 0 = none, – = little, + = some, ++ = much

Practice II: A Sample Character Across Narratives

4

To sample how we can profitably compare the same character in different narratives, we will consider the character of Jesus' mother in the four gospels.[14] In keeping with our discussion on the reader's knowledge (see chapter two), I hold that Mark was written first, Matthew used Mark, and Luke knew both Mark and Matthew. John also knew Mark but independently of Matthew and Luke.

Mark

Information about Mary in this gospel is sparse. In Mark 3.31–35, she is simply identified as the mother of Jesus and only in Mark 6.3 do we learn that her name is Mary. She hails from Nazareth (Mark 1.9) and has other children besides Jesus (Mark 3.32; 6.3). Jesus' father gets no mention, so Mary might have been a widow. Having heard concerning reports about her son's mental state, Mary and her family go in search of him to take charge of him (Mark 3.21, 31). Jesus' family outside is contrasted with those inside who sit around Jesus (Mark 3.31–35), and the next chapter continues to stress the contrast between outsiders and insiders (Mark 4.10–11). The association of Jesus' family with the scribes in the Beelzebul controversy, and their shared opinion of Jesus—'he is out of his mind' (Mark 3.21) and 'he is demon-possessed' (Mark 3.22), do nothing to improve Mary's characterization.

Nor does, possibly, her final appearance in the passion narrative. While there is a certain Mary among the women present at Jesus' crucifixion (Mark 15.40; see also 15.47; 16.1), it is far from certain that it is the same Mary mentioned in Mark 6.3. Most scholars think that they are different women. But even if this Mary in the passion and resurrection narratives is the same one in Mark 6.3 and Mark 3.31–35, she is not identified as the mother of *Jesus*, perhaps indicating that she is still an outsider. Besides, this Mary shows fear rather than faith and remains silent rather than proclaiming (Mark 16.7–8). If we discount her narrative presence in Mark 15–16, Mary never speaks, displays no traits, shows no development and her inner life is indiscernible. If she does have a narrative presence in Mark 15–16 (and this remains uncertain), she shows (conflicting) traits of loyalty (Mark 15.41), devotion (Mark 16.1) and inaction (Mark 16.8), and Mary's inner life would contain fear and bewilderment (Mark 16.8). In sum, if Mary is absent from the passion and resurrection narratives, she is simply an agent; if she is present, she may be classified as a 'type.'

Matthew

This gospel's unique contribution to Mary's characterization is the infancy narrative in Matthew 1–2, where she has a significant narrative presence. On closer analysis, however, Mary appears passive, flat and surprisingly anonymous. Her first mention is in the genealogy of Jesus as his mother (Matt 1.16). Jewish genealogies are mostly patrilineal and women rarely feature, but Matthew's genealogy mentions no less than five women—four are Gentile women (Tamar, Rahab, Ruth, Bathsheba) and one a Jewish woman (Mary). While Mary is co-opted into God's plan for Israel as the Messiah's mother, her association with these other women and their alleged immoral reputations could taint her characterization—though Matthew quickly quashes any possible misunderstanding in Matt 1.18–25.[15] Throughout the infancy narrative, Mary does not speak and is a passive figure—announcements are made about her and events happen to her. In Matthew 2, Mary is incidental to Joseph's actions, indicated by the recurring phrase 'the child and his mother' (Matt 2.13–14, 20–21).

Matthew also portrays Mary and her family as outsiders but softens the Markan portrait by leaving out Mark 3.21 where Mary and her family perceive Jesus as mentally unstable and by removing the negative association of Jesus' family with the scribes in the Beelzebul controversy. Hence, Matthew's contrast between Jesus' biological and spiritual family is less stark than in Mark. The Matthean passion and resurrection narratives show the same ambiguity regarding Mary's presence that we found in Mark. If we could place her there, and this is debatable, Mary would gain traits of loyalty (Matt 27.55). More significantly, however, Matthew would improve Mark's characterization of Mary at the empty tomb. Although Mary still displays fear, she also shows joy, devotion and responsiveness by proclaiming to the disciples what the angel and Jesus commission her to convey (Matt 28.7–11a).

While Matthew does not record Mary meeting the disciples, their presence in Galilee implies that she has conveyed Jesus' message (Matt 28.16). If Mary is present in Matthew 27–28, she shows traits of loyalty, devotion and responsiveness (Matt 28.9–11a). She would then show some development in having moved to Jesus' side after the events described in Matthew 12, without the ambiguity that surrounds Mary in Mark 15–16. Mary would also reveal aspects of her inner life, such as fear and joy. This would mean some complexity in terms of traits, some development and a little inner life, and I would classify Mary as a 'type' or 'personality'.

Luke

Like Matthew, Luke provides an account of Jesus' birth and childhood, but unlike Matthew, Luke presents Mary as an active, positive character from the start. While Matthew places Joseph in the foreground and Mary seems to be incidental, Luke reverses this. He portrays Mary as a young, intelligent, proactive mother who excels on every level. She has a profound grasp of her son's role in Israel's history, readily submits herself to God's purposes for Israel and expresses jubilant praise (Luke 1–2). Hence, Luke improves on Mary's characterization as seen in Matthew's birth narrative, but he also continues Matthew's softening of Mark's portrayal of Mary as being outside Jesus' circle of followers. First, Luke shortens the entire episode from five verses in Mark and Matthew to three verses (Luke 8.19–21). Secondly, Luke clarifies that the *crowd* causes Mary to remain outside, while Mark and Matthew leave open the possibility that she did not want to go inside (Luke 8.19).

Surprisingly, Mary has no narrative presence in Luke's passion and resurrection narratives. Yet, when we glance ahead to Luke's sequel, Mary makes another appearance, in Acts 1.14, where she is part of the early church after Jesus' ascension. In sum, Luke presents a rich characterization of Mary. She shows multiple traits and a rich inner life. Mary also shows development when she starts firmly on Jesus' side (Luke 1–2), then moves outside Jesus' circle (Luke 8.19–21), only to end up in Jesus' circle of followers again (Acts 1.14). Consequently, I position the Lukan Mary on the character continuum as one having 'personality', perhaps even moving to being an 'individual'.

John

In the Johannine narrative, Jesus' mother is an anonymous character—John nowhere mentions her name. Jesus' mother has a significant narrative presence on just two occasions—at the beginning and end of Jesus' ministry (John 2.3–5; 19.25–27).

At a wedding celebration, Jesus' mother witnesses the symbolic inauguration of her son's messianic ministry. In fact, she plays a key role in precipitating this remarkable event because of her powers of observation, her implicit request to Jesus and her instruction to the servants to obey Jesus' word (John 2.3–5).[16] In short, she is a catalyst for the start of Jesus' ministry. The second narrative appearance of Jesus' mother is at the foot of the cross in John 19.25–27. While we could interpret this event symbolically as the inception of the church, I suggest that Jesus fulfils his filial obligations with a practical solution—he institutes a new earthly family consisting of his mother and his dearest disciple. Knowing that he will no longer be able to care for his mother, he provides a home for her with his closest disciple. At the same time, when Jesus addresses his mother as 'woman' it is possibly meant to put some distance between them (see also John 2.4). Knowing he is returning to his Father, Jesus can no longer maintain links with this world or his biological family.[17]

The connection between John 2.3–5 and John 19.25–27, then, is the issue of filial obligations. Jesus addresses his mother as 'woman' on both occasions, indicating that his loyalty lies primarily with his family 'from above.' At the wedding in Cana, Jesus distances himself from his mother's plans because his primary concern is his Father's mission—though he also fulfils his filial obligations to his mother. At the cross, Jesus fulfils his filial obligations to his mother but once again distances himself from his family 'below' in order to return to his Father 'above'.

In sum, Jesus' mother is an uncomplicated character with some traits—she is practical, observant, caring and shows initiative. She shows no development and reveals nothing of her inner life. Hence, I put her on the character continuum as a 'type'.

Summary

The following table shows the aggregate information about Mary. Since her narrative presence at the cross and tomb in Mark and Matthew is in doubt, I have placed information that depends on such presence in brackets.

Jesus' Mother	Complexity	Development	Inner Life	Degree of Characterization
Mark	0 (or –)	0 (or –)	0 (or –)	agent (or type)
Matthew	0 (or +)	– (or +)	0 (or –)	agent (or personality)
Luke	+/++	–/+	++	personality/individual
John	+	0	0	type

Key: 0 = none, – = little, + = some, ++ = much

The quality of Mary's narrative presence is poor in Mark. Even if she were present at the cross and tomb, Mark gives mixed signals about her. While Matthew improves on Mark's characterization of Mary by adding the birth narrative and softening Mark's portrayal of Mary during Jesus' ministry, he does not do enough to make it unambiguous. Only if she were present at the cross and tomb, does the balance tip in her favour.

Luke and John both provide positive but different characterizations of Jesus' mother. While Luke achieves this by looking at the events before and beyond Jesus' ministry, John does so by focusing on the beginning and end of Jesus' ministry. Both improve significantly on Mark's characterization of Mary but independently of each other. Luke portrays Mary very positively within the infancy narrative, and although he retains the tension between Jesus' biological and spiritual family, he places Mary (back) on Jesus' side in Acts 1.14. John uniquely keeps Jesus' mother on Jesus' side throughout his narrative, in contrast to Jesus' brothers (see John 2.12 and John 7.1–9), whereas Mark contrasts Jesus' mother and brothers with Jesus' spiritual family.

When the same character appears in different narratives, a uniform method stimulates synchronic readings (that is, readings across narratives) and provides a basis for comparing the different characterizations. Instead of a composite of Mary reconstructed piecemeal from the four gospels, readers should recognize and appreciate how each gospel author presents Mary and her distinct role in each narrative.

5 A Final Word

When reading the gospels, we inevitably create mental pictures of the characters we encounter in the text. In this study, I have tried to show that we can be more intentional about how we reconstruct characters. This approach to character reconstruction provides guidelines for how readers can study the characters in the gospels. The uniform approach to character reconstruction has two benefits. First, it provides a nuanced and guided reconstruction of characters, and enables a comparison of characters within and across narratives. Secondly, it highlights the ongoing significance or representative value of characters, thus potentially shaping the reader's character and behaviour. For some, this approach to character will be sufficient (for example, in preparing for sermons or small group talks), but others might like to know whether this approach has more potential—I believe it has. Elsewhere, I have explored how characters serve the gospel authors' theology in a few short studies—on missiology in Mark, socioeconomic ethics in Luke and virtue ethics in John.[18]

Further Reading

C Bennema, *A Theory of Character in New Testament Narrative* (Minneapolis, MN: Fortress, 2014)

C Bennema, *Encountering Jesus: Character Studies in the Gospel of John* (Minneapolis, MN: Fortress, second edition, 2014)

F E Dicken and J A Snyder (eds), *Characters and Characterization in Luke-Acts* (New York: T and T Clark, 2016)

S A Hunt, D F Tolmie and R Zimmermann (eds), *Character Studies in the Fourth Gospel: Narrative Approaches to Seventy Figures in John* (Grand Rapids, MI: Eerdmans, 2016)

C W Skinner (ed), *Characters and Characterization in the Gospel of John* (New York: T and T Clark, 2013)

C W Skinner and M R Hauge (eds), *Character Studies and the Gospel of Mark* (New York: T and T Clark, 2014)

Notes

1 This is evident in S A Hunt, D F Tolmie and R Zimmermann (eds), *Character Studies in the Fourth Gospel: Narrative Approaches to Seventy Figures in John* (Grand Rapids, MI: Eerdmans, 2016) where all forty-four contributors choose their own approach.

2 Flat characters or 'types' have a single trait and do not develop. Round characters are complex, have multiple traits and can develop (*ie* surprise the reader).

3 C Bennema, *A Theory of Character in New Testament Narrative* (Minneapolis, MN: Fortress, 2014).

4 See F W Burnett, 'Characterization and Reader Construction of Characters in the Gospels,' *Semeia* 63 (1993): 3–28.

5 Ewen's works are in Hebrew but his theory is summarized in S Rimmon-Kenan, *Narrative Fiction: Contemporary Poetics* (New York: Methuen, 1983) pp 41–42.

6 For this refinement, I am indebted to M Bal, *Narratology: Introduction to the Theory of Narrative* (Toronto, ON: University of Toronto Press, 1985) pp 86–88.

7 If there is no protagonist, for instance in many Old Testament narratives (although God may be the protagonist), characters can be evaluated according to the author's point of view and purpose.

8 For aligning my character descriptors with ancient topics, I am indebted to A D Myers, *Characterizing Jesus: A Rhetorical Analysis on the Fourth Gospel's Use of Scripture in Its Presentation of Jesus* (New York: T and T Clark, 2012).

9 K S O'Brien, 'Written That You May Believe: John 20 and Narrative Rhetoric,' *CBQ* 67 (2005): 284.

10 D A Lee, 'Partnership in Easter Faith: The Role of Mary Magdalene and Thomas in John 20,' *JSNT* 58 (1995): 47–48.

11 C Bennema, 'The Identity and Composition of οἱ Ἰουδαίων in the Gospel of John,' *TynB* 60 (2009): 239-263. Sometimes, individuals can break out of their group identity: *eg* 'chief priest' Caiaphas in John 11.49, the believing 'Jews' in John 11.45 or the authorities (probably chief priests) in John 12.42.

12 J V Brownson, 'Neutralizing the Intimate Enemy: The Portrayal of Judas in the Fourth Gospel,' *SBL Seminar Papers* 31 (1992): 52.

13 See C Bennema, *Encountering Jesus: Character Studies in the Gospel of John* (Minneapolis, MN: Fortress, 2014).

14 For a detailed analysis, see C Bennema, 'Character Reconstruction in the New Testament (2): The Practice,' *ExpTim* 127 (2016): 417–429.

15 R E Brown *et al* (eds), *Mary in the New Testament* (New York: Paulist Press, 1978) p 84.

16 A Fehribach, *The Women in the Life of the Bridegroom* (Collegeville, MN: Liturgical Press, 1998) p 37.

17 B R Gaventa, *Mary: Glimpses of the Mother of Jesus* (Edinburgh: T and T Clark, 1999) p 91.

18 C Bennema, 'Gentile Characters and the Motif of Proclamation in the Gospel of Mark,' in C W Skinner and M R Hauge (eds), *Character Studies and the Gospel of Mark*, pp 215–231; *idem*, 'The Rich are the Bad Guys: Lukan Characters and Wealth Ethics,' in F Dicken and J Snyder (eds), *Characters and Characterization in Luke-Acts*, pp 95–108; *idem*, 'Virtue Ethics in the Gospel of John: The Johannine Characters as Moral Agents,' in L D Chrupcala (ed), *Rediscovering John* (Milan: Terra Santa, 2013) pp 167–181. These are freely available on lst.academia.edu/CornelisBennema